MASTERING UBUNTU

A Comprehensive Guide to Linux's Favorite Distribution

Ghada Atef

To my family, who have always supported and encouraged me to pursue my dreams. Without their love and unwavering support, this book would not have been possible.

"Ubuntu is a complete Linux-based operating system, freely available with both community and professional support. Ubuntu is suitable for both desktop and server use. It is user-friendly, with strong support for multimedia, and contains everything needed for daily use."

MARK SHUTTLEWORTH, FOUNDER OF UBUNTU

CONTENTS

PREFACE

Welcome to "Mastering Ubuntu: A Comprehensive Guide to Linux's Favorite Distribution". This book is designed to provide readers with a complete understanding of Ubuntu, one of the most popular Linux distributions used by millions of people worldwide.

Ubuntu is a powerful and versatile operating system that can be used for a wide range of applications, from running servers to powering desktop computers. It is known for its ease of use, robust security features, and excellent hardware support.

This book is for both new and experienced users who want to learn how to master Ubuntu. It covers a wide range of topics, from installation and configuration to advanced system administration, network setup, and security.

I begin with an introduction to Ubuntu and its features, followed by a step-by-step guide to installation and initial setup. I then move on to cover system administration, including managing users, groups, and permissions, working with the file system, and troubleshooting common issues.

The book also includes chapters on network setup and configuration, web server setup, and database administration. I cover topics like package management, software installation, and security, so readers can be confident in their ability to use Ubuntu in a professional environment.

Throughout the book, I provide practical examples and real-world scenarios to help readers understand the concepts and apply them to their own projects.

I hope this book will help readers gain a comprehensive understanding of Ubuntu and become proficient in using it in their daily tasks. Whether you are a developer, system administrator, or just a curious user, this book will help you take full advantage of Ubuntu's features and capabilities.

INTRODUCTION

Ubuntu is one of the most widely used Linux distributions in the world, favored by developers, system administrators, and desktop users alike. It is known for its ease of use, stability, and robust security features, making it an excellent choice for both personal and professional use.

"Mastering Ubuntu: A Comprehensive Guide to Linux's Favorite Distribution" is a book that provides readers with a complete understanding of Ubuntu, from installation and configuration to advanced system administration, network setup, and security. This book is designed for both new and experienced users who want to learn how to master Ubuntu and make the most of its features and capabilities.

In this book, I will guide readers through the process of installing and configuring Ubuntu, covering everything from choosing the right hardware to setting up the system for optimal performance. I will also delve into advanced topics like package management, software installation, and security, helping readers become proficient in using Ubuntu for their daily tasks.

I aim to provide readers with a practical, hands-on guide to using Ubuntu, complete with real-world examples and scenarios to help them understand the concepts and apply them to their own projects. By the end of this book, readers will have a comprehensive understanding of Ubuntu and be able to use it confidently in a professional environment.

I hope this book will be a valuable resource for anyone looking to master Ubuntu and become proficient in using this powerful and versatile operating system.

PROLOGUE

Linux has come a long way since its inception in 1991. Over the years, it has grown to become one of the most popular operating systems in the world, with a wide range of distributions catering to every need and use case. Ubuntu is one such distribution, known for its user-friendly interface, robust security features, and excellent hardware support.

As Linux has gained popularity, so has Ubuntu. It has become a go-to choice for developers, system administrators, and desktop users. Thanks to its ease of use, versatility, and stability. However, mastering Ubuntu requires a deep understanding of its features and capabilities. That is what this book aims to provide!

"Mastering Ubuntu: A Comprehensive Guide to Linux's Favorite Distribution" is a book designed to help readers understand Ubuntu, from installation and configuration to advanced system administration, network setup, and security. This book is for both new and experienced users who want to become proficient in using Ubuntu for their daily tasks.

I will begin with an introduction to Ubuntu and its features, followed by a step-by-step guide to installation and initial setup. I will then delve into topics like package management, software installation, and security, helping readers become proficient in using Ubuntu in a professional environment.

Throughout the book, I will provide practical examples and real-world scenarios to help readers understand the concepts and apply them to their projects. I aim to provide a comprehensive guide to using Ubuntu, complete with all the knowledge readers need to become proficient in using this powerful and versatile operating system.

I hope readers will find this book a valuable resource as they embark on their journey to mastering Ubuntu. Whether you are a developer, system administrator, or just a curious user, this book will help you take full advantage of Ubuntu's features and capabilities and become proficient in using it for your daily tasks.

FOREWORD

Ubuntu is a popular Linux distribution that has gained widespread use among developers, system administrators, and desktop users. Its ease of use, robust security features, and excellent hardware support have made it a top choice for many users worldwide.

"Mastering Ubuntu: A Comprehensive Guide to Linux's Favorite Distribution" is a book that provides readers with a complete understanding of Ubuntu and how to use it to its fullest potential. The book is written clearly and concisely, making it accessible to both new and experienced users.

As an experienced Linux user, I can attest to the importance of having a comprehensive guide to using Ubuntu. This book covers a wide range of topics, from installation and configuration to advanced system administration, network setup, and security, providing readers with all the knowledge they need to master Ubuntu.

What I particularly appreciate about this book is the practical examples and real-world scenarios provided throughout the text. These examples make it easy for readers to understand the concepts and apply them to their projects, helping them gain confidence in using Ubuntu for their daily tasks.

The authors have done an excellent job covering all the essential topics, from the basics to the advanced, making this book a valuable resource for anyone looking to become proficient in using Ubuntu. I highly recommend "Mastering Ubuntu: A Comprehensive Guide to Linux's Favorite Distribution" to anyone looking to learn more about this popular Linux distribution and become a power user.

Moustafa Elgezery, Linux Expert, and Data Scientist

CONTACTING ME!

You can reach me at *linux.expert.eg@gmail.com*. Please include the title of the book in the subject of your email.

CONTENTS

o Setting up web servers, databases, and email services
o Managing users, permissions, and resources
Chapter VII: Ubuntu for Developers
o Programming languages and development tools in Ubuntu
o Setting up development environments and workflows
o Version control with Git and other tools
o Building and packaging software for Ubuntu
Chapter VIII: Ubuntu for Cloud Computing
o Overview of Ubuntu cloud computing solutions
o Deploying and managing virtual machines and containers
o Setting up cloud storage and networking
o Scaling and managing cloud applications
Chapter IX: Conclusion
o Future directions and trends for Ubuntu
o Resources for further learning and support
Chapter X: Summary
o Summary

CHAPTER I: INTRODUCTION TO UBUNTU

I f you're new to the world of Linux, you may have heard of a distribution called Ubuntu. But what is Ubuntu, exactly? In this chapter, we'll introduce you to Ubuntu and show you how you can use it to get the most out of your computer.

So, let's get started and begin our journey of mastering Ubuntu!

I.I History and philosophy of Ubuntu

What is Ubuntu?

Ubuntu is a free and open-source Linux distribution. It is one of the most popular Linux distributions in the world, but its success is not just due to its technical features. Ubuntu has a unique history and philosophy that sets it apart from other operating systems. In this section, we'll explore the history and philosophy of Ubuntu and see how they've shaped the development of this powerful operating system.

History of Ubuntu

Ubuntu was first released in 2004 by Canonical Ltd., a company founded by South African entrepreneur Mark Shuttleworth. Shuttleworth's vision for Ubuntu was to create a Linux distribution that was easy to use, highly customizable, and accessible to everyone. Ubuntu was initially based on the Debian distribution, but over the years, it has developed into its unique operating system.

One of the defining moments in Ubuntu's history was the release of version 10.04 in 2010. This version, known as "Lucid Lynx," introduced the Unity interface, which was designed to be more user-friendly and intuitive than previous versions of Ubuntu. Unity received mixed reviews at first, but it helped establish Ubuntu as a serious contender in the world of operating systems.

Philosophy of Ubuntu

Ubuntu's philosophy is based on the concept of "humanity to others." This philosophy is reflected in the operating system's slogan, "Linux for human beings." The goal of Ubuntu is to create an operating system that is not only powerful and customizable but also easy to use and accessible to everyone.

One of the ways that Ubuntu embodies this philosophy is through its commitment to open-source software. Ubuntu is built on open-source software, which means that anyone can view and modify the source code. This makes it easier for developers to create new software and fix bugs, which helps make Ubuntu more stable and secure.

Another way that Ubuntu embodies its philosophy is through its commitment to inclusivity. Ubuntu is available in over 55 languages, which makes it accessible to people all over the world. Additionally, Canonical Ltd. has a code of conduct that emphasizes respect, collaboration, and inclusivity. This code of conduct is designed to create a welcoming and inclusive community around Ubuntu.

Conclusion

Ubuntu's history and philosophy have helped shape the development of this powerful operating system. From its humble beginnings in 2004 to its current status as one of the most popular Linux distributions in the world, Ubuntu has always been guided by a commitment to accessibility, inclusivity, and open-source software. Whether you're a newcomer to Linux or an experienced user, Ubuntu is a powerful and user-friendly operating system that can help you get the most out of your computer.

I.II Benefits of using Ubuntu

Ubuntu is one of the most popular Linux distributions available today, and for good reason. This powerful operating system offers a host of benefits to users, from increased security to greater customizability. In this section, we'll explore the benefits of using Ubuntu and see why it's such a popular choice among Linux users.

1. Increased Security

Ubuntu is known for its security features, which make it an excellent choice for anyone concerned about online security. The operating system is designed to be more secure than other operating systems like Windows or macOS. Ubuntu is built on open-source software, which means that the code is open for anyone to review and make changes to. This helps identify and fix security vulnerabilities more quickly than in closed-source operating systems.

2. Customizability

One of the greatest benefits of using Ubuntu is its customizability. The operating system is highly configurable, which means that you can tailor it to your specific needs. You can change everything from the appearance of the desktop to the behavior of the mouse. Additionally, Ubuntu's software center allows you to install and remove applications quickly and easily.

3. Cost-Effective

Ubuntu is a cost-effective alternative to other operating systems like Windows or macOS. The operating system is available as a free download, and many applications for Ubuntu are also free. This can help reduce costs for individuals and organizations that use

Ubuntu.

4. Stability and Reliability

Ubuntu is known for its stability and reliability. The operating system is less prone to crashes and other errors than other operating systems, which can save users time and frustration. Additionally, Ubuntu receives regular updates and security patches, which helps keep the operating system running smoothly.

5. Large and Active Community

Ubuntu has a large and active community of users and developers. This means that there are many resources available for users, including forums, blogs, and tutorials. Additionally, Ubuntu's community is known for being friendly and welcoming, which makes it easy for users to get help and support when they need it.

Conclusion

Ubuntu offers a host of benefits to users, from increased security to greater customizability. Whether you're a newcomer to Linux or an experienced user, Ubuntu is a powerful and user-friendly operating system that can help you get the most out of your computer. If you're looking for a cost-effective, stable, and reliable operating system with a large and active community, then Ubuntu is worth considering.

I.III Overview of Ubuntu versions and releases

Ubuntu is one of the most popular Linux distributions available today. It's known for its user-friendly interface, security features, and customizability. But, with so many different versions and releases of Ubuntu available, it can be difficult to keep track of them all. In this section, we'll give you an overview of the different Ubuntu versions and releases so you can choose the right one for your needs.

Ubuntu Releases

Ubuntu is released twice a year, in April and October. Each release has a version number that consists of the year and month of its release. For example, Ubuntu 20.04 was released in April 2020, Ubuntu 21.10 was released in October 2021, and Ubuntu 22.04 was released in April 2022.

There are two types of Ubuntu releases: Long Term Support (LTS) releases and non-LTS releases. LTS releases are supported for five years, while non-LTS releases are supported for nine months. LTS releases are intended for enterprise use, while non-LTS releases are ideal for home users and developers who want to stay up to date, with the latest software.

Ubuntu Versions

There are several versions of Ubuntu, each designed for different use cases:

1. Ubuntu Desktop: This is the most popular version of Ubuntu, designed for desktop and laptop computers. It comes with the GNOME desktop environment and includes a variety of pre-installed software, including the LibreOffice suite, Firefox web browser, and the

Rhythmbox music player.

2. Ubuntu Server: This version is designed for use as a server operating system. It includes a variety of tools for managing servers, including the popular LAMP (Linux, Apache, MySQL, and PHP) stack.
3. Ubuntu Cloud: This version is designed for use with cloud computing services like Amazon Web Services (AWS) and Microsoft Azure. It includes tools for managing cloud instances and supports a variety of cloud platforms.
4. Ubuntu Core: This version is designed for use with Internet of Things (IoT) devices. It's a lightweight operating system that includes only the essential components needed to run IoT devices.
5. Ubuntu Studio: This version is designed for multimedia content creators. It includes a variety of pre-installed multimedia software, including the Ardour digital audio workstation and the Blender 3D modeling software.

Conclusion

Ubuntu is a powerful and versatile operating system that's suitable for a wide range of users and use cases. Whether you're a home user, a developer, or an enterprise, there's an Ubuntu version that's right for you. By understanding the different Ubuntu releases and versions, you can choose the right one for your needs and get the most out of this powerful operating system.

CHAPTER II: INSTALLING UBUNTU

Installing Ubuntu is a straightforward process that involves downloading the Ubuntu image, creating a bootable USB drive, and then running the installer. Before you begin, it's important to back up any important files and ensure that your computer meets the system requirements for Ubuntu. Once you've completed these steps, you can start the installation process, which typically takes less than an hour. During the installation, you'll be prompted to choose your language, and timezone, and partition your hard drive, among other things. Once the installation is complete, you'll be able to start using Ubuntu and enjoy its many benefits.

II.I System requirements and hardware compatibility

Ubuntu is a popular Linux distribution that's known for its user-friendly interface, security features, and customizability. But, like any operating system, it has specific system requirements and hardware compatibility that users should be aware of. In this section, we'll go over the system requirements for Ubuntu and its compatibility with different types of hardware.

System Requirements

The minimum system requirements for Ubuntu vary depending on the version you're using. For example, Ubuntu 22.04 LTS requires a 2 GHz dual-core processor, 4 GB of RAM, and 25 GB of free hard drive space. However, these are just the minimum requirements, and you'll likely need more powerful hardware to run Ubuntu smoothly.

If you're planning to use Ubuntu for resource-intensive tasks like video editing or gaming, you'll want to make sure your hardware is up to the task. This may mean upgrading your RAM, installing a faster processor, or adding a dedicated graphics card. In general, the more powerful your hardware is, the better your Ubuntu experience will be.

Hardware Compatibility

Ubuntu is designed to work with a wide range of hardware, from desktop computers to laptops to servers. However, some hardware components may not be fully supported or may require additional configuration to work properly.

Graphics cards are one area where hardware compatibility can be an issue. Some graphics cards may not be fully supported by Ubuntu, which can result in graphical issues or poor performance. If you're planning to use Ubuntu for gaming or other graphics-intensive tasks, it's a good idea to check whether your graphics card is supported before installing Ubuntu.

Wireless network cards can also be a potential area of compatibility issues. While most wireless network cards will work with Ubuntu out of the box, some may require additional configuration or may not be fully supported. If you're planning to use Ubuntu on a laptop, it's a good idea to check whether your wireless network card is supported before installing Ubuntu.

Conclusion

Ubuntu is a powerful and versatile operating system that's suitable for a wide range of users and use cases. By understanding the system requirements and hardware compatibility of Ubuntu, you can ensure that your hardware is up to the task and that you'll be able to get the most out of this powerful operating system. Whether you're using Ubuntu for personal or professional use, having the right hardware is key to a great Ubuntu experience.

II.II Downloading and creating an installation media

Ubuntu is a popular Linux distribution that's known for its user-friendly interface, security features, and customizability. If you're interested in trying Ubuntu, one of the first things you'll need to do is download the Ubuntu image and create a bootable USB drive to install it. In this section, we'll go over the steps to download and create an installation media for Ubuntu.

Downloading the Ubuntu Image

The first step in installing Ubuntu is to download the Ubuntu image. You can download the latest version of Ubuntu from the official Ubuntu website. Once you're on the download page, select the version of Ubuntu you want to download and click the download button. The download may take a few minutes, depending on the speed of your internet connection.

Creating a Bootable USB Drive

Once you've downloaded the Ubuntu image, you'll need to create a bootable USB drive to install it. There are a few different tools you can use to create a bootable USB drive, but we'll go over the steps to create one using the free and open-source tool, Etcher.

1. Download and install Etcher from the official website.
2. Insert a USB drive with at least 4GB of free space into your computer.
3. Open Etcher and select the Ubuntu image you downloaded earlier.
4. Select the USB drive you inserted earlier.
5. Click the "Flash!" button to create the bootable USB drive.

Once Etcher has finished creating the bootable USB drive, you're ready to install Ubuntu on your computer.

Installing Ubuntu

To install Ubuntu, insert the bootable USB drive you created earlier into your computer and restart your computer. Your computer should automatically boot from the USB drive, but if it doesn't, you may need to change the boot order in your computer's BIOS settings.

Once Ubuntu has booted from the USB drive, you can follow the prompts to install Ubuntu on your computer. During the installation process, you'll be prompted to choose your language, and timezone, and partition your hard drive, among other things. Once the installation is complete, you'll be able to start using Ubuntu and enjoy its many benefits.

Conclusion

Downloading and creating an installation media for Ubuntu is a relatively straightforward process that can be done in just a few steps. By following the steps outlined in this section, you can quickly and easily create a bootable USB drive and install Ubuntu on your computer. Whether you're new to Ubuntu or an experienced user, having reliable installation media is key to a successful Ubuntu experience.

II.III Installation process and customization options

Ubuntu is a popular Linux distribution that's known for its user-friendly interface, security features, and customizability. If you're interested in installing Ubuntu on your computer, this section will walk you through the installation process and show you some of the customization options available.

Installation Process

To install Ubuntu on your computer, you'll need to create a bootable USB drive with the Ubuntu image and then boot your computer from the USB drive. Once you've booted from the USB drive, you'll be prompted to choose your language, time zone, and keyboard layout.

Next, you'll be prompted to select your installation type. You can choose to install Ubuntu alongside your existing operating system or replace it entirely. You'll also need to choose your partitioning scheme. If you're not sure which option to choose, the default option should be sufficient for most users.

After you've selected your installation type and partitioning scheme, you'll be prompted to create a user account and password. You'll also have the option to encrypt your home folder for added security.

Finally, you'll be prompted to confirm your installation settings before the installation process begins. The installation process may take a few minutes, depending on the speed of your computer and the size of your hard drive.

Customization Options

One of the great things about Ubuntu is the wide range of customization options available. Here are just a few of the ways you can customize your Ubuntu installation:

1. Desktop Environment: Ubuntu comes with the GNOME desktop environment by default, but you can choose to install a different desktop environment if you prefer. Some popular alternatives include KDE Plasma, XFCE, and Cinnamon.
2. Themes and Icons: You can change the look and feel of your Ubuntu desktop by installing themes and icons. There are many different themes and icons available in the Ubuntu Software Center, or you can download them from third-party websites.
3. Applications: Ubuntu comes with a wide range of pre-installed applications, but you can install additional applications to suit your needs. The Ubuntu Software Center makes it easy to browse and install new applications.
4. Terminal Customization: If you're a power user, you may want to customize your terminal to suit your needs. You can customize the appearance of your terminal, set up aliases, and even create custom scripts to automate tasks.

Conclusion

Installing Ubuntu on your computer is a straightforward process that can be done in just a few steps. Once you've installed Ubuntu, you'll have access to a wide range of customization options that allow you to tailor your Ubuntu experience to your needs. Whether you're a new user or an experienced Linux user, Ubuntu offers a powerful and customizable operating system that's worth checking out.

II.IV Dual-booting with other operating systems

Ubuntu is a popular Linux distribution that can be installed alongside other operating systems on the same computer. Dual-booting Ubuntu with another operating system, such as Windows or macOS, allows you to choose which operating system to use each time you boot your computer. In this section, we'll walk you through the process of dual-booting Ubuntu with another operating system.

Backup Your Data

Before you begin the dual-booting process, it's important to backup your data. Dual-booting can be a complex process, and there's always a risk of data loss or system damage. Make sure you have a backup of all your important files before proceeding.

Create a Bootable USB Drive

To install Ubuntu, you'll need to create a bootable USB drive with the Ubuntu image. You can use software like Rufus or UNetbootin to create a bootable USB drive.

Shrink Your Existing Partition

To create space for Ubuntu, you'll need to shrink the partition of your existing operating system. In Windows, you can do this by opening the Disk Management tool and right-clicking on your main partition, then selecting "Shrink Volume." In macOS, you can use the Disk Utility tool to resize your partition.

Create a New Partition

Once you've shrunk your existing partition, you'll need to create a new partition for Ubuntu. In Windows, you can do this by right-clicking on the unallocated space and selecting "New Simple

Volume." In macOS, you can use the Disk Utility tool to create a new partition.

Install Ubuntu

Insert your bootable USB drive and restart your computer. Boot from the USB drive, and follow the Ubuntu installation process. When prompted to choose your installation type, select "Install Ubuntu alongside [existing OS]." Ubuntu will automatically detect the free partition you created earlier and install itself there.

Configure Your Dual-Boot Options

After the installation process is complete, restart your computer. You should see a boot menu that allows you to choose which operating system to use. If you don't see a boot menu, you may need to configure your BIOS or UEFI settings to enable dual-booting.

Conclusion

Dual-booting Ubuntu with another operating system can be a great way to experience the benefits of both operating systems on the same computer. However, it's important to proceed with caution and backup your data before beginning the process. With the right tools and careful planning, dual-booting can be a smooth and seamless experience.

CHAPTER III:
GETTING STARTED
WITH UBUNTU

Getting started with Ubuntu can seem overwhelming at first, but it's quite straightforward. Ubuntu is a popular Linux distribution that is known for its ease of use and customizable interface. In this guide, we'll walk you through the basics of getting started with Ubuntu, including installation, customization, and common tasks like browsing the web and managing files. Whether you're a complete beginner or an experienced user, this guide will help you get up and running with Ubuntu in no time.

III.I Desktop environment and user interface

Ubuntu is a popular Linux distribution that is known for its user-friendly interface and customizable desktop environment. In this section, we'll take a closer look at the Ubuntu desktop environment and explore its various features and customization options.

Ubuntu Desktop Environment

The Ubuntu desktop environment is based on the GNOME desktop environment, which provides a modern, intuitive interface. The GNOME desktop environment features a panel at the top of the screen that provides access to the applications menu, system settings, and notifications. The panel also displays the current date and time, as well as the status of various system services.

Customizing the Desktop Environment

One of the strengths of Ubuntu is its ability to be customized to suit your individual needs and preferences. There are several ways to customize the Ubuntu desktop environment, including:

1. Changing the Wallpaper: You can change the background wallpaper of your desktop by right-clicking on the desktop and selecting "Change Desktop Background."
2. Installing Themes: You can install themes to change the overall look and feel of the desktop environment. Many websites offer free and paid themes for Ubuntu.
3. Adding Applets: Applets are small applications that run on the panel and provide quick access to system information and settings. You can add applets by right-clicking on the panel and selecting "Add to Panel."
4. Installing Extensions: GNOME extensions are small

add-ons that can be installed to add new features and functionality to the desktop environment. You can browse and install extensions from the GNOME Extensions website.

Using Applications

Ubuntu comes with a wide range of pre-installed applications, including the Firefox web browser, the LibreOffice office suite, and the Rhythmbox music player. You can also download and install additional applications from the Ubuntu Software Center or by using the command line.

Managing Files

The Ubuntu desktop environment includes the Nautilus file manager, which provides an easy-to-use interface for managing files and folders. You can use Nautilus to browse your files, create new folders, and copy, move, or delete files.

Conclusion

The Ubuntu desktop environment provides a user-friendly interface that is easy to use and customize. Whether you're a beginner or an experienced user, there are plenty of ways to make Ubuntu your own. By exploring the various customization options and learning how to use the built-in applications, you can get the most out of your Ubuntu desktop experience.

III.II Basic navigation and customization options

Ubuntu is a popular Linux distribution that offers a user-friendly interface and a range of customization options. Whether you're new to Ubuntu or an experienced user, this guide will help you get started with basic navigation and customization.

Basic Navigation

The Ubuntu desktop interface is based on GNOME, a modern and intuitive desktop environment. Here are some basic navigation tips to get started:

1. Applications Menu: To access the applications menu, click on the "Activities" button at the top left of the screen or press the "Super" key (usually the Windows key). From there, you can search for and launch applications.
2. Dock: The dock is a bar on the left side of the screen that provides quick access to your favorite applications. You can add or remove applications from the dock by right-clicking on an application and selecting "Add to Favorites" or "Remove from Favorites."
3. Workspaces: Workspaces are virtual desktops that allow you to organize your applications and windows. To switch between workspaces, use the "Ctrl + Alt + Arrow" keys or click on the workspaces button in the bottom right corner of the screen.

Customization Options

Ubuntu offers a range of customization options to make the desktop environment your own. Here are some of the most popular customization options:

1. Change the Desktop Background: To change the desktop background, right-click on the desktop and select "Change Desktop Background." From there, you can choose from a range of pre-installed wallpapers or upload your image.
2. Install Themes: You can install themes to change the appearance of the desktop environment. To install a theme, download the theme file and extract it to the ".themes" folder in your home directory. Then, use the GNOME Tweaks tool to apply the theme.
3. Add Extensions: GNOME extensions are small add-ons that can be installed to add new features and functionality to the desktop environment. You can browse and install extensions from the GNOME Extensions website.
4. Customize the Dock: You can customize the dock by right-clicking on an application in the dock and selecting "Preferences." From there, you can change the size and position of the dock, as well as add or remove applications.

Conclusion

By mastering basic navigation and exploring the range of customization options, you can create a personalized and efficient desktop environment in Ubuntu. Whether you prefer a minimalist or feature-rich interface, Ubuntu offers plenty of options to suit your needs.

III.III Installing and managing software packages

Ubuntu is a powerful and versatile operating system, offering a vast range of software packages for users to download and use. In this guide, we'll go over how to install and manage software packages in Ubuntu.

Package Management

Ubuntu uses the Advanced Package Tool (APT) for package management, which allows users to easily search for and install software packages. APT maintains a list of software packages available for Ubuntu, and can automatically resolve dependencies between packages.

Installing Packages

To install a package, open the terminal and use the following command:

```
$ sudo apt-get install package-name
```

Replace "package-name" with the name of the package you want to install. You will be prompted to enter your password to authorize the installation.

Updating Packages

To update the list of available packages, use the following command:

```
$ sudo apt-get update
```

To upgrade all installed packages, use the following command:

```
$ sudo apt-get upgrade
```

Removing Packages

To remove a package, use the following command:

```
$ sudo apt-get remove package-name
```

Replace "package-name" with the name of the package you want to remove. This will remove the package, but will not remove any configuration files associated with the package. To completely remove a package and its configuration files, use the following command:

```
$ sudo apt-get purge package-name
```

Searching Packages

To search for a package, use the following command:

```
$ apt-cache search package-name
```

Replace "package-name" with the name of the package you want to search for. This will return a list of packages that match your search term.

Managing Repositories

Ubuntu software packages are stored in repositories, which are online collections of software maintained by Ubuntu developers and third-party providers. To manage repositories, use the Software & Updates tool, which can be accessed from the Applications menu.

Conclusion

By mastering package management and exploring the vast range of software available for Ubuntu, you can take full advantage of the power and versatility of this operating system. Whether you're looking to install new software, keep your packages up to date, or manage repositories, Ubuntu offers plenty of tools and options to suit your needs.

III.IV Ubuntu Software Center

Ubuntu Software Center: Your One-Stop Shop for Software

The Ubuntu Software Center is a graphical user interface (GUI) that allows you to browse and install software on your Ubuntu system. But what exactly is the Ubuntu Software Center, and how can you use it to get the most out of your Ubuntu system? In this section, we'll take a closer look at the Ubuntu Software Center and explore some of its features.

What is the Ubuntu Software Center?

The Ubuntu Software Center is a GUI for the Advanced Packaging Tool (APT), which is the package management system used by Ubuntu and many other Linux distributions. APT is a command-line tool that allows you to install, remove, and manage software packages on your system. However, for those who prefer a graphical interface, the Ubuntu Software Center provides an easy-to-use alternative.

The Ubuntu Software Center is pre-installed on all Ubuntu systems, so you don't need to do anything to start using it. Simply open the Software Center from your Applications menu, and you'll be greeted with a user-friendly interface that allows you to browse and search for software packages.

Browsing and searching for software

The Ubuntu Software Center makes it easy to find the software you need. You can browse software by categories, such as Education, Games, or Graphics, or you can search for specific software by name or description. You can also view software by popularity, rating, or release date.

When you find a package that you're interested in, you can click on it to view more information about the package, including a description, screenshots, and user reviews. You can also see other related packages that may be of interest.

Installing and managing software

Once you've found the software package you want to install, simply click the "Install" button to begin the installation process. The Ubuntu Software Center will download and install the package for you, and you'll be notified when the installation is complete.

The Ubuntu Software Center also allows you to manage the software packages on your system. You can view a list of installed packages, remove packages that you no longer need, or upgrade packages to their latest versions.

Conclusion

The Ubuntu Software Center is a powerful tool that makes it easy to browse, search for, and install software on your Ubuntu system. With its user-friendly interface and wide selection of software packages, the Ubuntu Software Center is your one-stop shop for all your software needs.

So, if you're new to Ubuntu or just looking for an easier way to manage your software packages, give the Ubuntu Software Center a try. It's a great tool that can save you time and hassle, and help you get the most out of your Ubuntu system.

III.V Configuring system settings and preferences

Ubuntu offers a wide range of configuration options and settings that allow users to personalize their system and optimize it for their needs. In this guide, we'll go over some of the key system settings and preferences that you can configure in Ubuntu.

System Settings

To access the System Settings menu, click on the gear icon in the top right corner of the desktop and select "Settings". From here, you can configure a wide range of system settings, including:

- **Appearance:** customize your desktop theme, icons, fonts, and background.
- **Devices:** manage your printers, scanners, and other connected devices.
- **Displays:** configure your monitor settings, such as resolution, orientation, and refresh rate.
- **Power:** adjust power settings for your system, including battery and screen settings.
- **Sound:** manage your audio settings, including input and output devices, volume, and sound effects.
- **Users:** manage user accounts and settings, such as passwords and permissions.
- **Network:** configure your network settings, including Wi-Fi and Ethernet connections.

Additional settings and preferences can be accessed by clicking on the corresponding icons in the System Settings menu.

GNOME Tweaks

GNOME Tweaks is a powerful tool for customizing the GNOME desktop environment, which is the default desktop environment in Ubuntu. To install GNOME Tweaks, open the terminal and use the following command:

```
$ sudo apt-get install gnome-tweak-tool
```

Once installed, you can launch GNOME Tweaks from the Applications menu. From here, you can customize various settings, including:

- **Appearance:** customize window title bars, icons, and themes.
- **Desktop:** configure desktop icons, show/hide desktop icons, and tweak other related settings.
- **Extensions:** manage GNOME Shell extensions.
- **Fonts:** customize font settings, including the default font and font rendering.
- **Keyboard & Mouse:** configure keyboard and mouse settings, including shortcuts and gestures.
- **Top Bar:** customize the top bar of the desktop environment.

Conclusion

By taking advantage of the configuration options and settings available in Ubuntu, you can customize your system to meet your specific needs and preferences. From basic system settings to more advanced tweaks and customizations, Ubuntu offers plenty of options to help you get the most out of your operating system. With these tools and features at your disposal, you can create a personalized computing experience that is both powerful and user-friendly.

CHAPTER IV: COMMAND-LINE INTERFACE

T he command-line interface (CLI) is a powerful tool for interacting with Ubuntu and performing tasks that may not be possible through the graphical user interface (GUI). The CLI provides a text-based interface where you can enter commands and execute various tasks, such as navigating the file system, managing files and directories, and installing software packages. While the command-line interface may seem intimidating at first, it can be a valuable tool for power users and system administrators who want to perform tasks efficiently and quickly. In this guide, we'll cover some of the basics of the Ubuntu command-line interface and show you how to get started.

IV.I Terminal emulator
and shell basics

The terminal emulator is an essential part of the Ubuntu operating system, providing users with a command-line interface to interact with the system. The terminal emulator allows users to enter commands and run programs, providing access to powerful tools and utilities that can't be accessed through the graphical user interface. The shell is the program that interprets and executes the commands that are entered into the terminal emulator.

In Ubuntu, the default terminal emulator is called GNOME Terminal, which provides a powerful and flexible interface for interacting with the system. The terminal emulator is accessed by clicking on the Terminal icon in the Applications menu or by pressing the keyboard shortcut *Ctrl + Alt + T*.

The shell used by Ubuntu is called Bash, which stands for Bourne-again shell. Bash is a widely used shell and is the default shell in many Linux distributions, including Ubuntu. Bash provides a wide range of features and capabilities, including command history, command-line editing, and the ability to run scripts and automate tasks.

When you open the terminal emulator, you'll see a command prompt, which typically looks something like this:

username@hostname:~$

The prompt consists of several components, including the username, the hostname, and the current working directory. The tilde (~) symbol represents the home directory of the current user.

To enter a command, simply type it at the command prompt and press Enter. The shell will interpret the command and execute it, displaying the output on the screen. For example, you can use the ls command to list the contents of the current directory:

```
$ ls
```

You can also use various options and arguments with the ls command to customize its behavior. For example, the -l option displays the contents of the directory in a long format, including file permissions, ownership, and size:

```
$ ls -l
```

The terminal emulator also provides various keyboard shortcuts that can be used to navigate and edit the command-line. For example, you can use the up and down arrow keys to scroll through previously entered commands, or use *Ctrl + C* to cancel a running command.

In this section, we've covered some of the basics of the Ubuntu terminal emulator and Bash shell. With these fundamentals, you can start exploring the powerful tools and utilities available in the Ubuntu command-line interface.

IV.II Working with files and directories

One of the most important tasks in any operating system is working with files and directories. In Ubuntu, this is done primarily through the command-line interface using the terminal emulator and the Bash shell. In this section, we'll explore some of the basic commands and techniques for working with files and directories in Ubuntu.

Listing Directories and Files

To list the contents of a directory, you can use the ls command. For example, to list the contents of the current directory, simply type ls and press Enter:

```
$ ls
```

To list the contents of a specific directory, specify the directory path as an argument to the ls command. For example, to list the contents of the /home/user/Documents directory, type:

```
$ ls /home/user/Documents
```

Creating Directories

To create a new directory, use the mkdir command followed by the name of the new directory. For example, to create a new directory called myfolder, type:

```
$ mkdir myfolder
```

This will create a new directory called myfolder in the current working directory.

Creating Files

To create a new file, you can use the touch command followed by the name of the new file. For example, to create a new file called myfile.txt, type:

```
$ touch myfile.txt
```

This will create a new empty file called myfile.txt in the current working directory.

Moving and Renaming Files

To move a file to a different directory or rename it, use the mv command followed by the current filename and the new filename or directory path. For example, to move a file called myfile.txt to the /home/user/Documents directory, type:

```
$ mv myfile.txt /home/user/Documents/
```

To rename a file, simply specify the new filename instead of the directory path. For example, to rename myfile.txt to newfile.txt, type:

```
$ mv myfile.txt newfile.txt
```

Copying Files

To copy a file to a new location, use the cp command followed by the current filename and the new filename or directory path. For example, to copy a file called myfile.txt to the /home/user/ Documents directory, type:

```
$ cp myfile.txt /home/user/Documents/
```

Deleting Files and Directories

To delete a file, use the rm command followed by the filename. For example, to delete a file called myfile.txt, type:

```
$ rm myfile.txt
```

To delete a directory and all its contents, use the rm command with the -r option followed by the directory name. For example, to delete a directory called myfolder and all its contents, type:

```
$ rm -r myfolder
```

Conclusion

In this section, we've explored some of the basic commands and techniques for working with files and directories in Ubuntu. These are just a few of the many powerful tools and utilities available in the Ubuntu command-line interface, and mastering them can help you become a more proficient and efficient Ubuntu user.

IV.III Using commands and utilities for system administration

Ubuntu is a powerful operating system that offers a lot of flexibility and customization options. One of the key features of Ubuntu is its command-line interface (CLI), which allows users to perform various system administration tasks quickly and efficiently. In this section, we'll take a look at some of the most useful commands and utilities for system administration in Ubuntu.

1. apt-get

apt-get is one of the most popular command-line utilities in Ubuntu, and it's used for installing, updating, and removing software packages. With apt-get, you can quickly install new software packages or update existing ones with just a few commands.

To install a package, simply type:

$ sudo apt-get install <package_name>

For example, to install the popular text editor Vim, you would type:

$ sudo apt-get install vim

You can also use apt-get to update your system and installed packages:

$ sudo apt-get update
$ sudo apt-get upgrade

The first command updates the package lists, while the second command upgrades all installed packages to their latest versions.

2. systemctl

systemctl is a command-line utility used for managing system services and processes in Ubuntu. With systemctl, you can start, stop, and restart system services, as well as enable or disable them at boot time.

To start a service, type:

```
$ sudo systemctl start <service_name>
```

To stop a service, type:

```
$ sudo systemctl stop <service_name>
```

To restart a service, type:

```
$ sudo systemctl restart <service_name>
```

You can also use systemctl to enable or disable a service at boot time:

```
$ sudo systemctl enable <service_name>
$ sudo systemctl disable <service_name>
```

3. top

top is a command-line utility that provides real-time information about system processes and resource usage. With top, you can monitor CPU, memory, and disk usage, as well as view detailed information about running processes.

To launch top, simply type:

```
top
```

You can sort the process list by various criteria, such as CPU usage or memory usage, by pressing the corresponding keyboard shortcuts (e.g., press 'M' to sort by memory usage).

4. htop

htop is a more advanced version of top, with additional features and customization options. With htop, you can view detailed information about system processes, as well as perform various actions on them (e.g., send signals, kill processes, etc.).

To install htop, type:

`$ sudo apt-get install htop`

To launch htop, type:

`htop`

5. rsync

rsync is a command-line utility used for synchronizing files and directories between different systems or locations. With rsync, you can copy files, directories, and entire file systems, while preserving file attributes and permissions.

To use rsync, you'll need to specify the source and destination directories, as well as any additional options (e.g., to preserve file attributes, delete files that no longer exist, etc.).

Here's a basic rsync command to copy a directory from one location to another:

`rsync -avz <source_directory> <destination_directory>`

This will copy the contents of the source directory to the destination directory while preserving file attributes and permissions.

These are just a few of the many commands and utilities available for system administration in Ubuntu. With these tools, you can quickly and easily perform various system administration tasks, from installing and updating software packages to managing system services and processes.

IV.IV Shell scripting and automation

Shell scripting is an essential skill for Linux system administrators, and Ubuntu is no exception. In Ubuntu, the shell is the interface between the user and the operating system. It is a command-line interpreter that reads user input and executes commands. Shell scripts are sets of commands that are executed in sequence, and they can be used for automation, system administration, and other tasks.

The Ubuntu shell is called Bash (Bourne Again SHell). It is a powerful and flexible shell that supports a wide range of features, including variables, loops, conditionals, functions, and more. Bash scripts can be used to automate tasks such as backups, software installations, file processing, and system monitoring.

To create a Bash script in Ubuntu, you can use any text editor, such as Nano, Vim, or Emacs. The first line of a Bash script is called the shebang, and it specifies the interpreter that will be used to run the script. For example, the shebang for Bash is:

#!/bin/bash

This tells the system that the script should be executed using the Bash shell.

Once you have created your Bash script, you need to make it executable. You can do this by using the chmod command, which changes the file permissions. For example, to make your script executable, you can use the following command:

chmod +x script.sh

This will give the user permission to execute the script.
Some common tasks that can be automated using Bash scripts in Ubuntu include:

- **File processing:** Bash scripts can be used to perform batch operations on files, such as renaming, copying, moving, and deleting files.
- **System monitoring:** Bash scripts can be used to monitor system resources such as disk usage, memory usage, and CPU usage. This can be useful for detecting performance issues and optimizing system performance.
- **Backup and restore:** Bash scripts can be used to automate backup and restore operations, such as backing up files to a remote server or restoring files from a backup.
- **Software installation and updates:** Bash scripts can be used to automate software installation and updates, such as installing packages from the Ubuntu repositories or updating system packages.

Overall, shell scripting is an essential skill for Ubuntu users, and it can help to improve productivity and streamline system administration tasks. By learning how to create and use Bash scripts, Ubuntu users can become more proficient at using the command line and managing their systems.

CHAPTER V:
ADVANCED SYSTEM
ADMINISTRATION

As users become more comfortable with Ubuntu and its command-line interface, they may want to explore advanced system administration techniques. These techniques can include configuring network settings, managing storage devices, optimizing performance, and troubleshooting system issues. Advanced system administration also involves managing user accounts, securing the system, and implementing backups and disaster recovery plans. By learning these advanced techniques, Ubuntu users can become proficient in managing and customizing their systems to meet their specific needs.

V.I Managing system services and daemons

Ubuntu, like any other Linux distribution, relies on system services and daemons to perform various tasks in the background. These services and daemons are responsible for managing network connections, running scheduled tasks, managing hardware devices, and more. As an Ubuntu user, it's important to understand how to manage these services and daemons to ensure that your system runs smoothly.

Systemd is the default init system used in Ubuntu, and it provides a powerful set of tools for managing services and daemons. In this section, we'll cover some basic commands and techniques for managing services and daemons in Ubuntu.

Understanding Systemd

Systemd is an init system that is responsible for starting and managing system services and daemons. It replaces the traditional SysVinit system and offers many benefits, including the parallel startup of services, on-demand service activation, and better control over system resources.

Systemd uses unit files to define system services and daemons. These unit files are stored in the /etc/systemd/system/ directory, and they specify how a service or daemon should be started, stopped, and restarted. Unit files can also define dependencies between services and daemons, ensuring that they are started in the correct order.

Managing Services with Systemctl

Systemctl is the command-line utility used to manage services in Systemd. Here are some basic commands you can use to manage services:

- **systemctl status <service>:** Check the status of a service.
- **systemctl start <service>:** Start a service.
- **systemctl stop <service>:** Stop a service.
- **systemctl restart <service>:** Restart a service.
- **systemctl enable <service>:** Enable a service to start at boot.
- **systemctl disable <service>:** Disable a service from starting at boot.

For example, to start the Apache web server, you would run the following command:

```
$ sudo systemctl start apache2
```

Managing Daemons with Systemd

Daemons are long-running background processes that perform system tasks. Systemd manages daemons in the same way as services, using unit files to define how they should be started and stopped.

To manage daemons with Systemd, you can use the same commands as for services, but substitute "daemon" for "service". For example:

- **systemctl status <daemon>:** Check the status of a daemon.
- **systemctl start <daemon>:** Start a daemon.
- **systemctl stop <daemon>:** Stop a daemon.
- **systemctl restart <daemon>:** Restart a daemon.
- **systemctl enable <daemon>:** Enable a daemon to start at boot.
- **systemctl disable <daemon>:** Disable a daemon from starting at boot.

For example, to start the MySQL database daemon, you would run the following command:

```
$ sudo systemctl start mysql
```

Conclusion

Managing system services and daemons are an important part of maintaining an Ubuntu system. With Systemd, Ubuntu provides a powerful set of tools for managing services and daemons. By understanding how to use these tools, you can keep your system running smoothly and efficiently.

V.II Configuring networking and security settings

Ubuntu is a popular Linux distribution that offers a wide range of customization options for system administrators. One of the most important tasks of a system administrator is to configure networking and security settings. In this section, we will discuss some of the key aspects of Ubuntu networking and security.

Networking Configuration Ubuntu offers several tools and utilities to configure networking settings. One of the most commonly used tools is the NetworkManager. This tool allows you to manage network connections and settings from a graphical interface. You can easily configure wired and wireless connections, set up VPNs, and manage network proxies.

You can also use the command-line interface to manage networking settings. The ifconfig command allows you to view and configure network interfaces. The route command allows you to configure the routing table, which determines how network traffic is directed between different networks.

Another important aspect of networking configuration is DNS (Domain Name System) resolution. Ubuntu uses the /etc/resolv.conf file to configure DNS settings. You can manually edit this file to specify DNS servers or use the resolvconf utility to manage DNS settings.

Security Configuration Ubuntu offers several built-in security features that can be configured to enhance the security of your system. One of the most important features is the built-in firewall, known as ufw (Uncomplicated Firewall). ufw allows you to configure firewall rules to block or allow incoming and outgoing traffic.

Another important aspect of security configuration is user

management. Ubuntu allows you to create and manage user accounts, set passwords, and configure user permissions. You can also use the $ sudo command to allow certain users to run privileged commands.

Ubuntu also includes several utilities to help you manage security updates and patches. The apt-get command allows you to download and install software updates, including security updates. You can also use the unattended-upgrades package to automatically download and install security updates.

Conclusion

Configuring networking and security settings is an essential task for any Ubuntu system administrator. By using the tools and utilities built into Ubuntu, you can easily configure network connections, DNS resolution, firewall rules, user accounts, and security updates. With these tools, you can ensure that your Ubuntu system is secure and well-protected against cyber threats.

V.III Troubleshooting common issues and errors

Ubuntu is a powerful and reliable operating system, but like any software, it's not immune to problems. Whether you're a new user or a seasoned administrator, there are a few common issues that can crop up from time to time. In this post, we'll cover some of the most common Ubuntu issues and how to troubleshoot them.

1. **Slow performance:** One of the most frustrating issues you may encounter is slow performance. This can be caused by a variety of factors, such as low memory, a nearly full hard drive, or a CPU that's working too hard. To fix this issue, try closing any unnecessary applications or processes, and make sure you have enough free disk space. You can also try running the System Monitor application to identify any resource-hogging processes.

2. **Network connection problems:** If you're having trouble connecting to the internet or accessing network resources, it could be a problem with your network settings. Make sure your network adapter is properly configured and that you're using the correct IP address, subnet mask, and gateway settings. You can also try resetting your network connection or restarting your router.

3. **Software installation issues:** Sometimes you may run into problems when installing new software on Ubuntu. This can be due to missing dependencies or conflicts with existing software. To fix this issue, try using the Ubuntu Software Center to install software, as it will automatically resolve dependencies. If you're installing software from the command line, use the apt-get command with the -f option to fix any missing

dependencies.

4. **Boot problems:** If your Ubuntu system won't boot properly, it could be due to several issues. Common causes include a damaged or corrupted boot loader, file system errors, or hardware problems. To troubleshoot this issue, try booting into recovery mode and running a file system check. You can also try reinstalling the boot loader using the boot-repair tool.

5. **Display issues:** Finally, you may encounter issues with your display, such as a blank screen or incorrect resolution. This can be due to incorrect graphics driver settings or a hardware problem. To fix this issue, try adjusting your graphics settings or updating your graphics drivers.

These are just a few of the most common issues you may encounter when using Ubuntu. By understanding these issues and their causes, you can troubleshoot and resolve them quickly and easily. If you're ever stuck, don't be afraid to seek help from the Ubuntu community, as many knowledgeable users are happy to assist.

V.IV Backing up and restoring system data

Ubuntu is a reliable and stable operating system, but it is still essential to back up your data regularly. Backups help protect against data loss due to hardware failure, human error, malware, or other unforeseen circumstances. In this section, we will discuss the different backup strategies and tools available on Ubuntu.

Backup Strategies

Before diving into specific tools, it's essential to understand the different backup strategies available. The most common backup strategies are:

Full Backup

A full backup copies all the data in a system, including the operating system, installed software, user data, and settings. Full backups are useful for restoring a system to its previous state if it becomes corrupted or fails. However, full backups can be time-consuming and take up a lot of storage space.

Incremental Backup

An incremental backup only copies files that have changed since the last backup. This approach reduces backup time and storage requirements, but it requires more management and can take longer to restore than a full backup.

Differential Backup

A differential backup is similar to an incremental backup but only copies files that have changed since the last full backup. This approach reduces the backup time and storage requirements, but restoring data requires both the latest differential backup and the full backup.

Selective Backup

Selective backups are used to backup specific files or directories. This approach is useful for backing up critical data, but it requires manual management and can miss important files.

Backup Tools

Ubuntu includes several backup tools that can help automate and simplify the backup process. Here are some of the most popular backup tools on Ubuntu:

Timeshift

Timeshift is a system restore tool that creates incremental backups of the entire system. Timeshift can help restore the system to its previous state if it becomes corrupted or unstable. Timeshift is pre-installed in Ubuntu 18.04 and later versions.

Deja Dup

Deja Dup is a user-friendly backup tool that uses the duplicity backend. Deja Dup supports incremental backups, and it can encrypt and compress backups. Deja Dup is available in the Ubuntu Software Center.

Rsync

Rsync is a command-line utility that can synchronize files and directories between local or remote locations. Rsync supports incremental backups, and it can transfer only the changed data, which reduces backup time and storage requirements.

Borg Backup

Borg Backup is a powerful backup tool that supports

deduplication, compression, and encryption. Borg Backup is a command-line tool and requires some configuration, but it offers significant flexibility and control over the backup process.

Conclusion

In conclusion, backing up your data is an essential step in maintaining a reliable and stable system. Ubuntu offers several backup tools that can help automate and simplify the backup process, including Timeshift, Deja Dup, Rsync, and Borg Backup. Choose a backup strategy that suits your needs and budget, and remember to test your backups regularly to ensure they are working correctly.

CHAPTER VI: UBUNTU FOR SERVERS

U buntu is a popular operating system that is widely used in various fields, including server administration. Ubuntu Server is a variant of the Ubuntu operating system designed specifically for server use. It is a powerful and flexible platform that is highly customizable and can be used for a wide range of tasks, including web hosting, file serving, and database management. In this section, we will explore the various features and capabilities of the Ubuntu Server and how it can be used to set up and manage servers for your organization.

VI.I Ubuntu server editions and deployment options

Ubuntu is a popular Linux distribution that is widely used in server environments. Ubuntu Server is a variant of the Ubuntu operating system designed specifically for server use. In this section, we will explore the different editions of Ubuntu Server and the deployment options available.

Ubuntu Server Editions
Ubuntu Server is available in three main editions: LTS, Standard, and Minimal.

LTS Edition
The LTS (Long-Term Support) edition of Ubuntu Server is designed for enterprise use and is supported for five years from the date of release. This edition includes a stable release of Ubuntu with bug fixes and security updates. It is ideal for organizations that require stability and reliability over the long term.

Standard Edition
The Standard edition of Ubuntu Server is released every six months and is supported for nine months from the date of release. This edition includes the latest software updates and features and is ideal for organizations that require the latest technology and features.

Minimal Edition
The Minimal edition of Ubuntu Server is a stripped-down version of the operating system, with only the bare essentials required to run a server. This edition is ideal for organizations that require a lightweight and minimalistic operating system for their servers.

Deployment Options
Ubuntu Server can be deployed in several ways, including:

1. Installation on Physical Hardware Ubuntu Server can be installed on physical hardware, either as the primary operating system or as a virtual machine running on a hypervisor.
2. Cloud Deployment Ubuntu Server is available as an image on several cloud platforms, including Amazon Web Services, Google Cloud Platform, and Microsoft Azure. This allows organizations to easily deploy Ubuntu Server on cloud infrastructure and take advantage of the benefits of cloud computing, such as scalability and flexibility.
3. Container Deployment Ubuntu Server can also be deployed as a container using technologies such as Docker and Kubernetes. This allows organizations to easily deploy and manage applications in a containerized environment.

Conclusion

Ubuntu Server is a versatile and flexible operating system that can be used in a wide range of server environments. With its different editions and deployment options, organizations can choose the version of Ubuntu Server that best meets their needs and deploy it in the most suitable way for their environment.

VI.II Installing and configuring server applications

Ubuntu is a popular choice for server deployments due to its stability, security, and ease of use. In this section, we will explore how to install and configure server applications on Ubuntu.

Firstly, it is important to understand that there are two main editions of Ubuntu for server deployments: Ubuntu Server and Ubuntu LTS (Long-Term Support). The former is optimized for server use cases and comes with a minimal desktop environment, while the latter is designed for long-term support with security updates and bug fixes.

Once you have chosen your edition of Ubuntu, you can proceed with installing server applications. Ubuntu comes with a package manager called APT (Advanced Package Tool), which makes it easy to install software packages and their dependencies. You can use the command-line interface or a graphical package manager like Synaptic to install applications.

To install an application using APT, simply open a terminal and use the following command:

```
$ sudo apt-get install <package-name>
```

For example, to install the Apache web server, you would use the following command:

```
$ sudo apt-get install apache2
```

After the installation is complete, you can start and stop the server using the following commands:

```
$ sudo systemctl start apache2
$ sudo systemctl stop apache2
```

Other popular server applications that you can install on Ubuntu include MySQL or MariaDB for databases, Nginx or Lighttpd for web servers, and Postfix or Exim for email servers.

Once you have installed the application, you will need to configure it to work with your specific use case. Most server applications come with a default configuration file that you can modify to suit your needs. You can usually find the configuration files in the /etc directory.

For example, the Apache web server configuration file is located at /etc/apache2/apache2.conf. You can modify this file to change the server's settings, such as the default port, virtual hosts, and SSL certificates.

In addition to configuration files, server applications may also have log files that can help you diagnose issues. You can find the log files in the /var/log directory.

In conclusion, Ubuntu is a versatile operating system that can be easily deployed as a server. With the APT package manager and a vast selection of server applications available, you can quickly set up and configure your server to suit your needs.

VI.III Setting up web servers, databases, and email services

Ubuntu is a popular operating system for servers due to its stability, security, and ease of use. In this section, we will discuss how to set up web servers, databases, and email services on Ubuntu.

Web Servers

Apache and Nginx are the two most popular web servers on Ubuntu. Apache is known for its stability and extensive documentation, while Nginx is known for its performance and scalability.

To install Apache, run the following command:

```
$ sudo apt-get update
$ sudo apt-get install apache2
```

To install Nginx, run the following command:

```
$ sudo apt-get update
$ sudo apt-get install nginx
```

Once the installation is complete, you can start the web server with the following command:

```
$ sudo systemctl start apache2 # for Apache
$ sudo systemctl start nginx # for Nginx
```

To check if the web server is running, open a web browser and enter the IP address or domain name of the server. If everything is set up correctly, you should see the default Apache or Nginx welcome page.

Databases

MySQL and PostgreSQL are the two most popular databases on

Ubuntu. MySQL is known for its simplicity and ease of use, while PostgreSQL is known for its robustness and support for advanced features.

To install MySQL, run the following command:

```
$ sudo apt-get update
$ sudo apt-get install mysql-server
```

To install PostgreSQL, run the following command:

```
$ sudo apt-get update
$ sudo apt-get install postgresql
```

Once the installation is complete, you can start the database server with the following command:

```
$ sudo systemctl start mysql # for MySQL
$ sudo systemctl start postgresql # for PostgreSQL
```

To connect to the database server, you can use the command-line client or a graphical tool such as phpMyAdmin or pgAdmin.

Email Services

Postfix and Sendmail are the two most popular email servers on Ubuntu. Postfix is known for its ease of use and security, while Sendmail is known for its flexibility and support for complex configurations.

To install Postfix, run the following command:

```
$ sudo apt-get update
$ sudo apt-get install postfix
```

To install Sendmail, run the following command:

```
$ sudo apt-get update
$ sudo apt-get install sendmail
```

Once the installation is complete, you can start the email server with the following command:

```
$ sudo systemctl start postfix # for Postfix
$ sudo systemctl start sendmail # for Sendmail
```

To test the email server, you can send an email to an external email address and check if it is received.

Conclusion

In this section, we discussed how to set up web servers, databases, and email services on Ubuntu. While these are just the basics, they should give you a good starting point for configuring your Ubuntu server for your specific needs.

VI.IV Managing users, permissions, and resources

Managing users, permissions, and resources is an important aspect of system administration. In Ubuntu, there are various tools and commands available to manage users, permissions, and resources efficiently.

Managing Users

To manage users in Ubuntu, you can use the useradd, userdel, and usermod commands. These commands are used to create, delete, and modify user accounts, respectively.

To create a new user account, you can use the useradd command followed by the username. For example, to create a new user account called john, you can use the following command:

```
$ sudo useradd john
```

To delete a user account, you can use the userdel command followed by the username. For example, to delete the john user account, you can use the following command:

```
$ sudo userdel john
```

To modify a user account, you can use the usermod command followed by the username and the modification option. For example, to modify the john user account to change the home directory to /home/john2, you can use the following command:

```
$ sudo usermod -d /home/john2 john
```

Managing Permissions

In Ubuntu, file and directory permissions are managed using the chmod, chown, and chgrp commands.

The chmod command is used to change the permissions of a file or directory. Permissions are set using three digits: the first digit represents the owner's permissions, the second digit represents the group's permissions, and the third digit represents everyone else's permissions.

For example, to set the permissions of a file named file.txt to read, write, and execute for the owner, read-only for the group, and read-only for everyone else, you can use the following command:

$ sudo chmod 744 file.txt

The chown command is used to change the ownership of a file or directory. For example, to change the ownership of a file named file.txt to the user john, you can use the following command:

$ sudo chown john file.txt

The chgrp command is used to change the group ownership of a file or directory. For example, to change the group ownership of a file named file.txt to the group users, you can use the following command:

$ sudo chgrp users file.txt

Managing Resources

In Ubuntu, system resources such as CPU, memory, and disk space can be managed using various commands and tools.

The top command is used to display real-time information about system resources, including CPU and memory usage. To run the top command, simply type top in the terminal.

The free command is used to display information about memory usage and availability. To run the free command, simply type free in the terminal.
The df command is used to display information about disk usage and availability. To run the df command, simply type df in the terminal.

Conclusion

Managing users, permissions, and resources is an important aspect of system administration in Ubuntu. By using the tools and commands available in Ubuntu, you can efficiently manage users, permissions, and resources to keep your system running smoothly.

CHAPTER VII: UBUNTU FOR DEVELOPERS

U buntu for Developers is a version of the Ubuntu operating system that is optimized for software development. It includes a variety of pre-installed development tools and libraries, making it easier for developers to create and deploy software applications. Ubuntu for Developers also includes support for a range of programming languages, such as Java, Python, Ruby, and C++, as well as development environments like Eclipse and IntelliJ IDEA. Additionally, Ubuntu for Developers is designed to integrate with popular cloud platforms like AWS and Google Cloud, making it a popular choice for building and deploying cloud-based applications.

VII.I Programming languages and development tools in Ubuntu

Ubuntu is a popular operating system among developers, thanks to its wide range of programming languages and development tools. In this section, we'll take a look at some of the most popular programming languages and development tools available in Ubuntu.

Programming Languages

Python

Python is a high-level programming language that is easy to learn and has a large community of developers. Ubuntu comes with Python pre-installed, so developers can get started with Python right away. Python is popular for web development, scientific computing, data analysis, and machine learning.

Java

Java is a widely used programming language that is popular for developing web applications, mobile applications, and desktop applications. Ubuntu comes with OpenJDK, an open-source implementation of the Java Development Kit, pre-installed. Developers can also choose to install Oracle's Java Development Kit if needed.

JavaScript

JavaScript is a popular programming language for web development. Ubuntu comes with Node.js, a JavaScript runtime, and NPM, a package manager for Node.js, pre-installed.

C/C++

C and C++ are low-level programming languages that are

popular for developing system software, operating systems, and embedded systems. Ubuntu comes with the GNU Compiler Collection (GCC), a collection of compilers and libraries that supports C, C++, and other programming languages.

Ruby
Ruby is a high-level programming language that is popular for web development, scripting, and automation. Ubuntu comes with Ruby pre-installed, so developers can get started with Ruby right away.

Development Tools
Integrated Development Environments (IDEs)

Ubuntu supports a range of popular Integrated Development Environments (IDEs) for software development. Some of the most popular IDEs available in Ubuntu include:

- Visual Studio Code
- Eclipse
- NetBeans
- IntelliJ IDEA
- PyCharm
- Atom

Text Editors

Ubuntu also supports a range of text editors for software development. Some of the most popular text editors available in Ubuntu include:

- Vim
- Emacs
- Nano
- Sublime Text
- Gedit

Version Control Systems

Version control systems are essential tools for managing and tracking changes in software projects. Ubuntu supports a range of version control systems, including:

- Git
- SVN
- Mercurial
- Bazaar

Package Managers

Package managers are tools that allow developers to install and manage software packages easily. Ubuntu comes with the Advanced Package Tool (APT), a package manager that makes it easy to install, upgrade, and remove software packages. Developers can also use other package managers like Snap, Flatpak, and AppImage.

Conclusion

Ubuntu is a popular operating system among developers, thanks to its wide range of programming languages and development tools. Whether you're developing web applications, desktop applications, or system software, Ubuntu has the tools you need to get the job done. With its large community of developers and extensive documentation, Ubuntu is an excellent choice for developers of all levels of experience.

VII.II Setting up development environments and workflows

Ubuntu is a popular operating system choice for developers due to its stability, security, and open-source nature. Setting up a development environment in Ubuntu can be a straightforward process, and there are various tools and workflows available to streamline the development process. In this post, we will cover the essential steps to set up your development environment in Ubuntu and improve your workflow.

Step 1: Installing Required Software

Before starting with the development, you need to install the required software on your system. Ubuntu's software center and command-line package manager, apt, provide an extensive collection of software. Some of the essential software for development are:

- **Git:** Git is a version control system used to track changes in the codebase. It is an essential tool for any developer.
- **Python:** Python is a popular programming language with a vast community and an extensive library of packages.
- **Node.js:** Node.js is a JavaScript runtime built on the V8 engine. It allows developers to run JavaScript code outside of a web browser.
- **Text Editor:** A good text editor can save time and increase productivity. Some popular text editors for Ubuntu include VS Code, Atom, and Sublime Text.

Step 2: Setting up Your Development Environment

Once you have installed the necessary software, the next step is to set up your development environment. You can set up a local development environment or use a virtual machine or container. Some popular tools for setting up development environments include:

- VirtualBox: VirtualBox is an open-source virtualization software that allows you to run multiple operating systems on a single machine.
- Docker: Docker is a containerization platform that allows developers to package an application and its dependencies into a single container.

Step 3: Improving Your Workflow

After setting up your development environment, the next step is to improve your workflow. Some popular tools and techniques for improving your workflow include:

- **Integrated Development Environment (IDE):** An IDE is a software application that provides comprehensive facilities to computer programmers for software development. Some popular IDEs for Ubuntu include Eclipse, PyCharm, and Visual Studio Code.
- **Debugging Tools:** Debugging tools help developers identify and resolve errors in their code. Some popular debugging tools for Ubuntu include gdb and valgrind.
- **Version Control:** Version control tools help developers track changes in their codebase and collaborate with other developers. Git is the most popular version control system.
- **Automation Tools:** Automation tools automate repetitive tasks and save time. Some popular automation tools for Ubuntu include Ansible and Puppet.

In conclusion, setting up a development environment in Ubuntu can be a simple process. By installing the required software, setting up your development environment, and improving your workflow, you can create a streamlined development process.

Whether you are a beginner or an experienced developer, Ubuntu offers the tools and resources to build great software.

VII.III Version control with
Git and other tools

Version control systems are essential tools for any developer who wants to keep track of code changes and collaborate with others. One of the most popular version control systems is Git, which is widely used in the development community.

Ubuntu, being a popular Linux distribution, has built-in support for Git and other version control tools. In this section, we will explore how to set up and use Git on Ubuntu, as well as other version control tools that are available.

Setting up Git on Ubuntu

To use Git on Ubuntu, you first need to install it. The easiest way to do this is to use the package manager:

$ sudo apt-get install git

This will install the latest version of Git on your system.

After installing Git, you should configure your username and email address so that Git can properly identify you when you commit changes. You can do this by running the following commands:

$ git config –global user.name "Your Name"
$ git config –global user.email "youremail@example.com"

Using Git on Ubuntu

With Git installed and configured, you can now start using it to manage your code.

The first step is to create a new repository. You can do this by running the following command in the directory where you want to create the repository:

```
$ git init
```

This will create a new Git repository in the current directory.
Once you have created a repository, you can start adding files and
making changes. To add a file to the repository, you can use the
following command:

```
$ git add filename
```

To commit changes to the repository, use the following command:

```
$ git commit -m "commit message"
```

This will commit the changes and add a message describing the
changes you made.

Other version control tools

While Git is the most popular version control system, there are
other options available as well.

One such option is Subversion, which is also available on Ubuntu.
To install Subversion, you can use the following command:

```
$ sudo apt-get install subversion
```

Mercurial is another popular version control system that is
available on Ubuntu. To install Mercurial, use the following
command:

```
$ sudo apt-get install mercurial
```

Conclusion

Version control is an essential tool for developers, and Git is the
most popular version control system used today. With Ubuntu, it
is easy to set up and use Git, as well as other version control tools
like Subversion and Mercurial. By using version control, you can
keep track of changes to your code, collaborate with others, and
ensure that your code is always up-to-date and secure.

VII.IV Building and packaging software for Ubuntu

Ubuntu is a popular Linux distribution that provides a robust and stable platform for software development. One of the advantages of using Ubuntu is the availability of a large number of software packages that can be easily installed using the package management system. However, if you need to develop your software and distribute it to others, you'll need to learn how to build and package your software for Ubuntu.

Building Software for Ubuntu

Before you can package your software for Ubuntu, you need to build it. Building software involves compiling the source code and creating the executable program that can be run on Ubuntu. The steps involved in building software depend on the programming language you're using and the build system you've chosen.

Here are some general steps that you can follow to build your software for Ubuntu:

1. **Install the required development tools and libraries:** Depending on the programming language you're using, you may need to install compilers, interpreters, and other development tools. You'll also need to install any libraries that your software depends on.
2. **Download the source code:** If you're building software from source code, you'll need to download the source code for your project.
3. **Configure the build system:** Most projects use a build system like Make or CMake to automate the build process. You'll need to configure the build system to use the correct compilers and libraries.
4. **Build the software:** Run the build command to compile

the source code and create the executable program.

Packaging Software for Ubuntu

Once you've built your software, you'll need to package it so that it can be easily installed and distributed to others. Ubuntu uses a package management system called dpkg, which allows you to create and manage software packages.

Here are the basic steps involved in packaging software for Ubuntu:

1. **Create a Debian package:** A Debian package is a file that contains all the files and information needed to install your software. You can use a tool like dpkg-deb to create a Debian package from your compiled software.
2. **Create a package metadata file:** The Debian package format requires a metadata file that describes the package, its dependencies, and other information. You can create this file using a text editor or a tool like dh_make.
3. **Build the package:** Run the dpkg-buildpackage command to build the Debian package from the metadata file and the compiled software.
4. **Distribute the package:** Once you've built the package, you can distribute it to others. You can either distribute it directly, or you can upload it to a package repository like Launchpad or Ubuntu's official package repository.

Conclusion

Building and packaging software for Ubuntu can seem intimidating at first, but it's an essential skill for developers who want to distribute their software to Ubuntu users. By following the steps outlined in this section, you can build and package your software for Ubuntu and make it available to a wider audience.

CHAPTER VIII:
UBUNTU FOR CLOUD
COMPUTING

U buntu is a popular operating system choice for cloud computing due to its stability, security, and support for various cloud platforms. Ubuntu has a strong presence in the cloud computing industry, offering both public and private cloud solutions for businesses and individuals. With Ubuntu, users can easily deploy and manage cloud applications, access cloud-based tools and services, and leverage cloud infrastructure to scale their operations. Ubuntu also offers compatibility with popular cloud platforms such as AWS, Microsoft Azure, and Google Cloud, making it a versatile and reliable option for cloud computing.

VIII.I Overview of Ubuntu cloud computing solutions

Ubuntu is one of the most popular Linux distributions, known for its reliability, security, and ease of use. It's also a preferred choice for cloud computing due to its flexibility and scalability. In this section, we will take a look at the different Ubuntu cloud computing solutions available today.

1. Ubuntu Server

Ubuntu Server is a powerful and reliable operating system that is designed for servers. It's optimized for security and performance and comes with a range of tools and features that make it ideal for hosting websites, running applications, and managing data.

2. Ubuntu Cloud

Ubuntu Cloud is a cloud computing platform that enables you to create and manage your cloud infrastructure. It comes with a range of tools and features that make it easy to deploy and manage virtual machines, storage, and networking resources.

3. Ubuntu OpenStack

Ubuntu OpenStack is a cloud computing platform that is built on top of OpenStack, an open-source cloud computing software. It provides a complete set of tools and services for building private, public, and hybrid clouds. Ubuntu OpenStack is scalable, reliable, and flexible, making it an ideal choice for businesses of all sizes.

4. Ubuntu Containers

Ubuntu Containers is a lightweight and efficient way to run applications on a cloud infrastructure. It uses containerization technology to isolate applications and their dependencies, making them more portable and easier to manage. Ubuntu Containers can be deployed on any cloud infrastructure, including public, private, and hybrid clouds.

5. Ubuntu Serverless

Ubuntu Serverless is a cloud computing platform that enables you to run code without the need for servers. It's based on the serverless computing model, which means that you only pay for the computing resources that your code uses. Ubuntu Serverless is ideal for running small applications or microservices that don't require a lot of computing power.

In conclusion, Ubuntu offers a range of cloud computing solutions that cater to different needs and use cases. Whether you're running a small website or managing a large-scale cloud infrastructure, Ubuntu has the tools and features you need to get the job done.

VIII.II Deploying and managing virtual machines and containers

Ubuntu is a popular operating system for cloud computing, and it provides powerful tools and services for deploying and managing virtual machines and containers. With Ubuntu, you can easily create and launch virtual machines and containers to run your applications and services in the cloud.

Virtual Machines in Ubuntu

Ubuntu supports several virtual machine hypervisors, including KVM, VirtualBox, and VMware. KVM is the default hypervisor in Ubuntu and provides robust performance and scalability. To use KVM, you need to ensure that your CPU supports virtualization extensions, such as Intel VT-x or AMD-V.

To create a new virtual machine in Ubuntu, you can use the virt-manager tool, which provides a graphical user interface for managing virtual machines. With virt-manager, you can easily configure the virtual machine's hardware settings, such as CPU, memory, and storage, and install the guest operating system using an ISO image or network installation.

Once you have created a virtual machine, you can start, stop, and manage it using the virsh command-line tool. With virsh, you can also take snapshots of the virtual machine, clone it, and migrate it to another host.

Containers in Ubuntu

Ubuntu supports several container runtimes, including Docker, LXD, and Podman. Docker is the most popular container runtime and provides a simple and efficient way to package and deploy applications in containers.

To install Docker in Ubuntu, you can use the apt package manager or the official Docker repository. Once you have installed Docker, you can use the Docker command-line tool to build, run, and manage containers. With Docker, you can also create custom images for your applications and publish them to a Docker registry.

LXD is a container hypervisor that provides a more lightweight and secure environment for running containers. LXD uses system containers, which share the same kernel as the host operating system but provide a separate namespace for each container. This allows you to run multiple containers on the same host while ensuring that they are isolated from each other.

To use LXD in Ubuntu, you need to install the lxd package and configure the LXD daemon. Once you have configured LXD, you can use the lxc command-line tool to create, start, stop, and manage containers. With LXD, you can also create container profiles, which define the container's configuration, and container images, which can be used to launch new containers.

Conclusion

Ubuntu provides a powerful and flexible platform for deploying and managing virtual machines and containers in the cloud. With its support for multiple virtualization and containerization technologies, Ubuntu allows you to choose the right tool for your needs and create the optimal environment for your applications and services. Whether you are building a complex infrastructure or a simple web application, Ubuntu has the tools and services you need to succeed in the cloud.

VIII.III Setting up cloud storage and networking

Ubuntu is a popular operating system for cloud computing, thanks to its robust features, stability, and security. In this section, we'll discuss how to set up cloud storage and networking in Ubuntu.

Cloud Storage

Cloud storage is a storage model in which data is stored on remote servers that can be accessed via the internet. It allows you to store your data in a highly available and scalable manner. Here's how to set up cloud storage in Ubuntu:

1. **Choose a cloud storage provider:** There are several cloud storage providers, such as Amazon S3, Google Cloud Storage, and Microsoft Azure. Choose a provider that suits your needs and budget.
2. **Install the cloud storage client:** Most cloud storage providers offer a client application that you can use to access and manage your data. Install the client application on your Ubuntu machine.
3. **Configure the client:** After installing the client application, you need to configure it to connect to your cloud storage account. This typically involves providing your account credentials and setting up a local folder to sync with your cloud storage.
4. **Sync your data:** Once the client is configured, you can start syncing your data to the cloud storage. You can choose to sync all your data or only specific folders.

Networking

Networking is a critical aspect of cloud computing. You need to set up a reliable and secure network to ensure that your cloud-based applications and services are accessible to your users. Here's how to set up networking in Ubuntu:

1. **Choose a networking provider:** There are several networking providers, such as Amazon VPC, Google Cloud VPC, and Microsoft Azure Virtual Network. Choose a provider that suits your needs and budget.
2. **Configure the network:** After choosing a networking provider, you need to configure the network to suit your requirements. This typically involves setting up subnets, security groups, and routing tables.
3. **Connect to the network:** Once the network is configured, you need to connect your Ubuntu machine to the network. This can be done via a VPN or a direct connection.
4. **Configure firewall rules:** Finally, you need to configure firewall rules to ensure that your Ubuntu machine is secure and protected from external threats. You can use Ubuntu's built-in firewall or a third-party firewall solution.

Conclusion

Setting up cloud storage and networking in Ubuntu is a straightforward process that can be done in a few simple steps. By following the steps outlined in this section, you can ensure that your cloud-based applications and services are reliable, scalable, and secure.

VIII.IV Scaling and managing cloud applications

In recent years, cloud computing has become an increasingly important technology for businesses and organizations of all sizes. Ubuntu is a popular choice for cloud computing, offering a range of solutions for deploying, managing, and scaling cloud applications. In this section, we'll take a closer look at Ubuntu's capabilities in the cloud, and how it can help you build and scale your cloud-based applications.

Deploying and managing virtual machines and containers

One of the key advantages of Ubuntu for cloud computing is its support for virtual machines and containers. With tools like VirtualBox and LXD, you can easily deploy and manage virtual machines and containers on Ubuntu-based cloud platforms like Amazon Web Services (AWS) and Google Cloud Platform (GCP). This allows you to run multiple instances of your applications in a secure and isolated environment, without having to worry about conflicts or compatibility issues.

Setting up cloud storage and networking

Another important consideration for cloud computing is storage and networking. With Ubuntu, you have access to a wide range of tools for configuring and managing cloud storage and networking. For example, you can use tools like Ceph and GlusterFS to set up distributed storage systems that can scale to meet the needs of even the largest applications. You can also use tools like Open vSwitch and OpenStack Neutron to manage networking resources and configure complex network topologies.

Scaling and managing cloud applications

Finally, Ubuntu offers a range of tools and services for scaling and managing cloud applications. For example, tools like Juju and Kubernetes allow you to automate the deployment and scaling of your applications, so you can easily scale up or down as demand changes. You can also use tools like Nagios and Zabbix to monitor the performance of your applications and ensure that they are running smoothly.

Conclusion

In conclusion, Ubuntu offers a range of powerful tools and services for cloud computing, making it an ideal choice for businesses and organizations that need to build and scale cloud-based applications. Whether you're deploying virtual machines and containers, setting up cloud storage and networking, or scaling and managing your applications, Ubuntu has the tools and expertise you need to get the job done. So why not give it a try and see what Ubuntu can do for your cloud computing needs?

CHAPTER IX: CONCLUSION

IX.I Future directions and trends for Ubuntu

Ubuntu has been evolving and adapting to new technologies and trends over the years, and there are several interesting developments on the horizon. In this section, we will explore some of the future directions and trends for Ubuntu.

1. Snaps

Snaps are a new packaging format for Ubuntu, which allows developers to distribute applications with all their dependencies bundled in a single package. This makes it easier to install and update the software on Ubuntu systems and ensures that applications are always running with the correct dependencies. Snaps are also more secure, as they are sandboxed and isolated from other applications and the system.

2. IoT

Ubuntu is becoming increasingly popular in the Internet of Things (IoT) space. With its small footprint and support for a wide range of architectures, Ubuntu is well-suited for use in embedded devices and IoT gateways. Ubuntu Core, a version of Ubuntu designed specifically for IoT devices, offers a secure and reliable platform for building and deploying IoT applications.

3. AI and Machine Learning

Ubuntu is also gaining traction in the AI and machine learning space. With support for popular machine learning frameworks like TensorFlow, PyTorch, and Caffe, Ubuntu is a popular platform for building and training AI models. Ubuntu also offers tools for deploying and managing AI applications, such as Juju and Charmed Kubernetes.

4. Cloud Computing

Ubuntu is a popular choice for cloud computing, with many cloud providers offering Ubuntu images as part of their offerings. Ubuntu is also a popular platform for building and deploying cloud applications, with tools like Juju and Charmed Kubernetes making it easy to manage and scale cloud infrastructure.

5. Desktop

While Ubuntu's focus has largely been on the server and cloud computing spaces, the desktop version of Ubuntu remains popular among users. Ubuntu's user-friendly interface and large software repository make it a popular choice for both home and office use. Ubuntu 22.04 LTS, released in April 2022, introduced several new features and improvements, including a new dark mode, improved performance, and enhanced security features.

In conclusion, Ubuntu is a versatile and adaptable operating system that has been evolving to meet the needs of different industries and use cases. With its focus on security, reliability, and ease of use, Ubuntu is well-suited for use in a wide range of applications, from IoT devices to cloud infrastructure to desktop computers. As new technologies and trends emerge, Ubuntu is likely to continue evolving to meet the needs of developers and users.

IX.II Resources for further learning and support

Ubuntu is a versatile and powerful operating system that can be used for a variety of purposes, including desktop computing, server deployment, and cloud computing. Whether you are new to Ubuntu or have been using it for years, there are plenty of resources available to help you learn more about the system and get support when you need it.

In this section, we will cover some of the best resources for learning more about Ubuntu and getting help when you need it.

1. Ubuntu Documentation
The Ubuntu Documentation provides a comprehensive guide to using Ubuntu, including installation, customization, and administration. This resource is especially useful for new users who are just getting started with Ubuntu. The documentation is available online and can be accessed from the Ubuntu website.

2. Ubuntu Forums
The Ubuntu Forums are an excellent resource for getting help with Ubuntu. The forums are moderated by experienced Ubuntu users who are available to answer questions and provide support. The forums cover a wide range of topics, including installation, hardware compatibility, and software configuration.

3. Ask Ubuntu
Ask Ubuntu is a question-and-answer website for Ubuntu users. It is similar to other Q&A websites like Stack Overflow but is focused specifically on Ubuntu. You can ask questions about Ubuntu and get answers from other users who have

experience with the system. Ask Ubuntu is a great resource for troubleshooting issues and getting help with specific problems.

4. Ubuntu Community Help Wiki

The Ubuntu Community Help Wiki is a community-maintained resource that provides detailed information about using Ubuntu. The wiki covers a wide range of topics, including installation, configuration, and troubleshooting. The wiki is constantly updated by the Ubuntu community, so it is always up-to-date with the latest information.

5. Official Ubuntu IRC Channels

The Ubuntu community maintains several IRC channels where users can get help and support. These channels are monitored by experienced Ubuntu users who are available to answer questions and provide assistance. The channels cover a wide range of topics, including installation, hardware compatibility, and software configuration.

6. Ubuntu Mailing Lists

The Ubuntu community maintains several mailing lists where users can ask questions and get help. The lists cover a wide range of topics, including installation, configuration, and troubleshooting. Subscribing to these mailing lists is a great way to stay up-to-date with the latest Ubuntu news and get help when you need it.

7. Ubuntu Certified Professional Program

The Ubuntu Certified Professional program is a certification program for Ubuntu administrators and engineers. The program is designed to validate the skills and knowledge of Ubuntu professionals. The certification can help you demonstrate your proficiency with Ubuntu and increase your job prospects.

8. Ubuntu Conferences and Events

Ubuntu hosts several conferences and events throughout the year. These events are a great way to learn more about Ubuntu and meet other members of the Ubuntu community. The events cover a wide range of topics, including installation, configuration, and development.

9. Ubuntu Community

The Ubuntu community is a vibrant and active community of users and developers who are passionate about Ubuntu. The community is a great resource for learning more about Ubuntu and getting help when you need it. The community is always happy to welcome new members, so don't be afraid to get involved.

IX.III Conclusion

In conclusion, Ubuntu is a powerful and versatile operating system that can be used for a wide range of purposes, from desktop computing to cloud computing and development. Its user-friendly interface and extensive package management system make it easy to use and customize, while its robust security and stability make it a reliable choice for mission-critical applications.

Whether you're a casual user looking for a reliable and easy-to-use desktop environment, a developer looking for a versatile development platform, or an IT professional looking for a powerful and scalable cloud computing solution, Ubuntu has something to offer. With its strong community support and commitment to open-source principles, Ubuntu is likely to remain a leading choice for users and organizations around the world for years to come.

If you're interested in learning more about Ubuntu, there are many resources available, including online documentation, forums, and user groups. Whether you're just getting started or you're a seasoned user, there's always something new to learn and discover in the world of Ubuntu.

CHAPTER X: SUMMARY

X.I Summary

Mastering Ubuntu is a comprehensive guide to one of the most popular Linux distributions in the world. The book is designed for both beginners and experienced users, and it provides a thorough overview of Ubuntu from installation and configuration to advanced system administration, server management, and cloud computing.

The book covers all aspects of Ubuntu. It starts with an introduction to Ubuntu and its history, followed by an explanation of the installation process and basic usage of the desktop environment. It then delves into more advanced topics such as shell scripting, system administration, server deployment, and cloud computing. The book also covers programming languages and development tools in Ubuntu, including version control with Git and packaging software for Ubuntu.

Throughout the book, readers will find practical examples, tips, and tricks that will help them become more productive and efficient with Ubuntu. The book is designed to be an essential reference for anyone using Ubuntu, whether for personal or professional purposes.

By the end of the book, readers will have a deep understanding of Ubuntu and its capabilities, and they will be able to use Ubuntu to its fullest potential. Whether readers are new to Ubuntu or experienced users, Mastering Ubuntu is the ultimate guide to mastering this powerful and versatile Linux distribution.

EPILOGUE

I hope you have found "Mastering Ubuntu: A Comprehensive Guide to Linux's Favorite Distribution" a valuable resource in your journey to mastering Ubuntu. This book provides readers with a complete understanding of Ubuntu, from installation and configuration to advanced system administration, network setup, and security.

I aimed to provide practical, hands-on guidance to help readers understand Ubuntu's features and capabilities and apply them to their projects. I have covered all the essential topics, from package management and software installation to network setup and security. To provide readers with a comprehensive guide to using Ubuntu for their daily tasks.

I understand that the world of Linux can be overwhelming at times, but I hope this book has helped make the learning process easier. My goal was to provide a clear and concise guide to using Ubuntu, and I believe we have achieved that goal.

In closing, I would like to thank you for choosing "Mastering Ubuntu: A Comprehensive Guide to Linux's Favorite Distribution" as your guide to Ubuntu. I hope that this book has helped you become proficient in using this powerful and versatile operating system and that you continue to explore all that Ubuntu has to offer.

ABOUT THE AUTHOR

Ghada Atef

As a Linux expert, author, and online instructor, I am passionate about sharing my knowledge and skills with others and empowering them to succeed in their pursuits. With over twelve years of experience in the industry, I have honed my expertise in areas such as Linux administration, IT automation, and Scripting.

As an author, I have published six books on topics ranging from Linux administration to IT automation. And as an online instructor, I have created two online courses that have helped students worldwide to learn and grow.

I prioritize integrity, excellence, innovation, collaboration, and impact. I am committed to providing the highest quality, professionalism, and value to my clients, readers, and students.

Overall, I dedicate myself to using my skills and expertise to make a positive impact worldwide, and I am excited to continue growing and learning in my work.

BOOKS BY THIS AUTHOR

Unofficial Red Hat Certified System Administrator Rhcsa 8 & 9 (Ex200) Exam Preparation: Six Complete Rhcsa 8 & 9 Practice Exams With Answers

Are you looking to become a Red Hat Certified System Administrator? Look no further than "Unofficial Red Hat Certified System Administrator RHCSA 8 & 9 (EX200) Exam Preparation"! This comprehensive exam preparation guide includes six complete practice exams with detailed answers, giving you the tools you need to confidently pass the RHCSA 8 & 9 exam.

Whether you're a seasoned IT professional or just starting your career, this book will help you master the skills necessary to become a Red Hat Certified System Administrator. With its practical, real-world approach and focus on the latest exam objectives, you'll be well-prepared to tackle any challenge that comes your way.

Get ahead of the competition and prove your expertise in Linux system administration with "Unofficial Red Hat Certified System Administrator RHCSA 8 & 9 (EX200) Exam Preparation". Start your journey towards certification success today!

Unofficial Rhcsa 8 & 9 (Ex200) Complete Reference: Rhel 8 & 9

Looking for a comprehensive guide to help you become a Red Hat Certified System Administrator? "Unofficial RHCSA 8 & 9 (EX200) Complete Reference: RHEL 8 & 9" is the perfect book for you! This all-in-one reference is packed with everything you need to know to master the skills required to become an RHCSA.

With a focus on Red Hat Enterprise Linux 8 & 9, this book covers everything from basic Linux commands to advanced system administration tasks. Whether you're a beginner or an experienced professional, you'll find the information you need to succeed.

Written by an experienced IT professional, this guide includes practical examples and hands-on exercises to help you put your new skills into practice. With its clear and concise explanations and up-to-date information, "Unofficial RHCSA 8 & 9 (EX200) Complete Reference: RHEL 8 & 9" is the only reference you'll need to prepare for the RHCSA exam.

Start your journey towards becoming a Red Hat Certified System Administrator today! Order "Unofficial RHCSA 8 & 9 (EX200) Complete Reference: RHEL 8 & 9" now and take the first step towards a successful career in IT.

Mastering Ansible: A Comprehensive Guide To Automating Configuration Management And Deployment

Are you looking for a comprehensive guide to mastering Ansible? Look no further than "Mastering Ansible: A Comprehensive Guide to Automating Configuration Management and Deployment". This book is the ultimate resource for anyone who wants to learn how to automate configuration management and deployment using Ansible.

With its clear and concise explanations, practical examples, and hands-on exercises, "Mastering Ansible" will help you become an expert in no time. Whether you're a beginner or an experienced professional, this book has everything you need to know to get the most out of Ansible.

Written by an experienced IT professional, this guide covers everything from the basics of Ansible to advanced topics like creating custom modules and using Ansible with Docker. With its focus on practical, real-world applications, "Mastering Ansible" is the perfect resource for anyone who wants to automate their IT infrastructure.

So what are you waiting for? Order "Mastering Ansible: A Comprehensive Guide to Automating Configuration Management and Deployment" today and take the first step towards becoming an Ansible expert!

Bash Scripting: Learn To Automate Your Tasks

Do you want to automate your daily tasks and improve your productivity? "Bash Scripting: Learn to Automate Your Tasks" is the perfect guide for you! This comprehensive book will teach you everything you need to know about Bash scripting, from the basics of scripting to advanced techniques for automating complex tasks.

With its clear and concise explanations, practical examples, and hands-on exercises, "Bash Scripting" will help you become an expert in no time. Whether you're a beginner or an experienced programmer, this book has something for everyone.

Written by an experienced IT professional, this guide covers everything from basic scripting concepts to advanced topics like writing functions and using regular expressions. With its focus on practical, real-world applications, "Bash Scripting" is the perfect resource for anyone who wants to automate their tasks and improve their productivity.

So what are you waiting for? Order "Bash Scripting: Learn to Automate Your Tasks" today and take the first step towards becoming a Bash scripting expert!

Learn Python Essentials: For Newbie Python Developers & Data Scientists

Are you a newbie Python developer or data scientist looking to master the essentials of Python? Look no further than "Learn Python Essentials"! This comprehensive guide is the perfect resource for anyone who wants to learn Python from scratch and become proficient in this powerful programming language.

With its clear and concise explanations, practical examples, and hands-on exercises, "Learn Python Essentials" will help you become an expert in no time. Whether you're a beginner or an experienced programmer, this book has something for everyone.

Written by an experienced IT professional, this guide covers everything from basic Python concepts to advanced topics like data manipulation and visualization. With its focus on practical, real-world applications, "Learn Python Essentials" is the perfect resource for anyone who wants to become a Python developer or data scientist.

So what are you waiting for? Order "Learn Python Essentials" today and take the first step towards mastering Python and unlocking its full potential!

THANK YOU!